THE **Seed**

MANIFESTO
BOOK

www.seedfusion.com

Two trees will be planted for every one used in the production of this book

THE Seed

MANIFESTO BOOK

the *feminine* way to create business

Lynne Franks

Thorsons

Thorsons
An Imprint of HarperCollins*Publishers*
77-85 Fulham Palace Road,
Hammersmith, London W6 8JB

The Thorsons website address is: www.thorsons.com

First published 2001
10 9 8 7 6 5 4 3 2 1

A catalogue record of this book
is available from the British Library

ISBN 0 00 711614 4

Printed and bound in Great Britain by
Martins The Printers Limited, Berwick upon Tweed

ACKNOWLEDGEMENTS

I would like to thank my collaborator and friend Michael Bockman, who co-developed the SEED manifesto with me so eloquently into a philosophy to inspire women and men all over the world.

INTRODUCTION

There is a revolution going on in the world and it's coming from the grass roots. It's the revolution of the sustainable entrepreneurs, mainly women, and it's about personal growth as well as an economic tool. It's political with a small p and it's organic, not structured. It's about creating value, developing relationships, and being financially empowered.

It's the feminine way to create business.

... and every revolution needs a manifesto, so welcome!

Lynne x

Seed MANIFESTO

I, ... , *affirm that I will*

Constantly plant seeds as well as pick the blooms

Keep the space and time to stay in tune with my higher self

Never let go of the big vision

Put my values, including integrity, compassion
and love, at the center of my enterprise

Remember the three R's: respect for self, respect
for others, responsibility for all my actions

Believe in myself so others will too

Keep humor and laughter as vital

ingredients of my business plan

Get up early in the morning

Not neglect my personal relationships,

loved ones, and friends in any way

Manifest abundance in all areas of my life

Keep my clutter to a minimum

Recognize my gifts and delegate the rest

Look at difficult situations from all perspectives

Welcome in mentors and mentor others in return

Light candles every day and surround myself with fresh flowers

Give people more than they expect

Talk slowly but think quickly

When I lose, don't lose the lesson

Know my industry

Keep improving my technology skills

Smile when picking up the phone

Remember my body is my most important tool –
stretch, exercise, breathe, go for a walk, dance

Every day try and read a poem, listen to an inspiring piece

of music, look at a wonderful painting or go into nature

●

Drink six to eight glasses of pure water every day

●

Listen as well as talk

●

Learn the rules then break some

●

Know there is nothing more sexy than confidence

●

Remember that no-one, not even I am

perfect, but I'm doing the best I can

●

SIGNED..

Date.........................

CONSTANTLY PLANT SEEDS AS WELL AS PICK THE BLOOMS

Starting something new, whether a life change, a relationship, a business, is very much like planting a garden. You have to nurture the seeds – the new ideas, the new hopes, the new dreams – and while they germinate you need to know what to do to allow them to bloom into a healthy plant. Starting something new should be organic, something that grows naturally from who you are as a person.

As planting seeds is about new life springing up, so a new personal direction or enterprise is also about the renewal of life. And like renewing the soil with mulch and compost, you should look at your new endeavour with the idea of sustainability – that it will constantly replenish itself as it continues to grow.

Sustainability is an old way of gardening and a new way of approaching life and business. It's based in the belief that an enterprise should be built on one's passions and commitment as well as profit. It means that your values to life, to the environment and to human and social rights are incorporated into the daily way your business operates. Sustainability has little to do with getting rich quick, but everything to do with leading a value-filled, rewarding life, both materially and spiritually.

It is important to enjoy the rewards of your labours, to pick the flowers that you have sown. It is equally important to keep your garden and life continually blooming — to always be aware of the replenishing process and how to maintain a healthy garden and life.

Take a look at how you can include the idea of sustainability into your new direction or business. Personalise it. Ask yourself what kind of gardener you are. What are your passions and what are your gifts? What are your values and how can you incorporate them in your work and life? Planting your seeds is about taking responsibility for your own life, working and living by the values that are important to you. Once you do this, your garden will bloom far more beautifully than it ever has.

KEEP THE SPACE AND TIME TO STAY IN TUNE WITH MY HIGHER SELF

We cannot bring in the new until the old is cleared out. Before a garden can be seeded, the ground has to be prepared. The rocks and weeds need clearing, the earth has to be turned and the nutrients introduced.

Starting a business or any new project in your life is the same. You have to create the right environment to be able to grow your vision. By clearing the physical disorder around you, you open up your space for new growth to come in. Similarly, by setting the priorities in life, you are able to eliminate the clutter and focus on what really matters.

Make a list of your priorities in order of importance, then put that list in a drawer. Look at it a month later. Are your priorities still the same? Has the urgency of some faded? This will help give you an idea of what tasks you should be tackling.

Setting plans and priorities is only part of the preparation. To find your way to your higher self, to finally hear your intuitive voice clearly, you have to clear your inner space as well.

It is important to take time to be away from the noise of your daily life. Finding quiet time must become an essential part of your daily routine if you truly hope to access your inner voice.

Create a special place where you can have your quiet time. Making an altar in your home is easy: cover a small table with a beautiful piece of cloth and place special objects and pictures representing your dreams and loved ones on it.

By just relaxing there, letting your mind be free and unencumbered in your special space, thoughts will begin drifting through. Trust that your unconscious mind is working at the deepest level to give you the tools you need to bring your garden to life. You'll be surprised how effectively this works.

Of course, life is full of distractions with families, jobs and friends. If you can only spend 10 minutes of every day in your special place, ideas will begin to germinate and your dreams will start to grow.

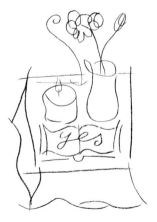

NEVER LET GO OF THE BIG VISION

Some gardens start off carefully planned, blueprinted by landscape architects and planted with careful precision. Other gardens are created in a spontaneous, improvisational manner. Similarly, some people know exactly what they want, have a plan all mapped out and know their final destination before they begin. Others think they know where they're going, but are not sure of how to get there. Still others feel uncertain of their goal, vision or enterprise.

Wherever you are, it is important to find your inner voice and listen to its truth. Is this the vision you really want? If you are choosing a new career or life path, is it the one that truly excites you? Or perhaps there is something else that fits in far better with your personal values, passions and skills.

Do your research. Yes. Logically think about the reality of your choices. Of course. But the SEED way is to 'feel' first.

Create a SEED vision poster on an 18" by 24" poster board, with images and words of your vision. Let the inspiration for this come to you. Take quiet time in a special place or at your altar for meditation. Ask for guidance from the creator to be in touch with your innermost thoughts and dreams. And then create.

Cut out magazine images, stick on photographs of you, loved ones, pets; write words that resonate with you, that make you feel good. A collage will take shape and a vision that encompasses your dreams and passions will appear.

Sit with it. Let it grow. Keep adding to it.

And be flexible with it. As there is always more than one solution to a problem, there is always more than one business in your area of interest and more than one path to your destination. Don't be afraid to explore all possibilities within your vision.

Obstacles and roadblocks are part of the process. Don't be discouraged when things get difficult. When situations become too overwhelming, take a break for a while. Let go of control and allow things to develop naturally. Trust that your initial instincts were right. The details may change, but if your vision is true for you, following it will be the most rewarding gift you can give yourself.

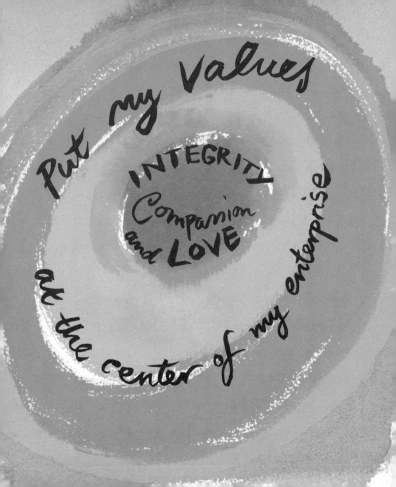

PUT MY VALUES, INCLUDING INTEGRITY, COMPASSION AND LOVE, AT THE CENTER OF MY ENTERPRISE

Wouldn't it be more enjoyable to work in a way that is sympathetic with your inner belief system? Why shouldn't you incorporate the values and moral principles of your daily life into your work life? We lose a crucial part of ourselves when we don't act on what we deeply believe or don't practise what we preach – in our work place as well as our home. For far too long the traditional business paradigm of profit and 'winning at all costs' has been all that mattered. A new paradigm is emerging, a more feminine paradigm, where such business practices as honesty, integrity and love are incorporated into the way business is done.

Companies large and small are starting to find that it works. A profit can be made while still maintaining principles and values that treat people with proper respect and dignity.

The challenge is to create a holistic life for yourself where there is no separation between work values and personal values. When your values and life are integrated, then work changes from a labour of drudge to a labour of love. You'll find yourself full of energy and far more healthy. Putting your values at the center of your enterprise will revitalise your body and spirit.

It takes persistence to change well ingrained habits and behavioural patterns. Begin today with a few simple steps. Ask yourself and make a list of your answers: What are your personal values? How would you prioritise them? Which values influence almost every decision you make in your life? Which keep your inner being in balance? And how do these values relate to your business ethics and to the way you intend to interact with people and the marketplace?

Take that list and put it over your desk. Read those values every day. Think about how you can put them into practice. They are the guideposts by which you'll create both a successful business and a happy life.

REMEMBER THE THREE R's: RESPECT FOR SELF, RESPECT FOR OTHERS, RESPONSIBILITY FOR ALL MY ACTIONS

Respect is one of the key ingredients to a successful business and life. It begins with respecting yourself. Respecting the values you live by and the skills that have brought you to this point. We often take for granted the uniqueness of our path and the abilities that we have learned that serve us daily. During a quiet time in your special place or at your altar, reflect on the events, the teachers and the experiences, both good and bad, that have shaped you into the unique person you are. Look at your strengths and weaknesses, honestly assess your passions and skills. Isn't it amazing how complex and rich a background you have? Take a moment to respect and give thanks to all that has made you into the person you are.

As you begin to respect yourself, you can respect others as well, because every person comes through life with a similar richness and complexity. And they are as unique as you are, with backgrounds that are different and skills that are wide and varied. A skill you may be lacking in may be another's strength. When working with others, it is essential to know their strengths and weaknesses as well as yours. Respect towards others only strengthens your team.

Similarly, whenever a conflict may arise, respect of the other person is the most important skill you can have for conflict resolution. It allows you to see things from their point of view. Once you take your ego away from the conflict and see their side, a win-win solution is more easily attained.

In business as in life, it is essential to take ultimate responsibility for your actions. It is easy to blame others or circumstances for an action you took. But, on closer examination, it is only you that made the decision. And it must be you who lives by the consequences. There is a cause and effect to every action; your decisions do make an impact. Think deeply and chose wisely before deciding to act. If you act through integrity, there will never be a need to deny responsibility.

BELIEVE in MYSELF

So others will TOO

BELIEVE IN MYSELF SO OTHERS WILL TOO

The truth is we can do anything we want – it's our own doubts and lack of self-confidence that hold us back. In creating and running a business, having confidence and self-esteem is essential. From raising start-up funds to leading a work force, you have to have the confidence in your vision and abilities or no one else will.

And we all have that confidence! It's just a matter of finding it.

You'd be surprised how much courage you are already using in daily life and don't give yourself credit for. Just getting up in the morning and dealing with your day can take an enormous amount of courage. Look back at your day today and make a list of the things you did that took a lot of courage for you.

And then take it a step further. Dare yourself to do something you fear. It shouldn't have anything to do with work, but should be an activity that you would always regret you never tried. Ideally, you should do it in a week. Dare to get in the habit of being daring.

What are we so afraid of?

For many, standing up and being seen is a big fear. If that's the case, the next time you are in a situation where you can be seen, make it a point to prepare yourself as much as possible and push yourself forward. If you speak and act from the heart, your fear will melt away.

Confrontation is another big fear. And the longer you put off confrontation, the harder it is. Again, if you stay true to yourself and come from a place of grace rather than anger, a confrontation, no matter how uncomfortable, will almost always take a turn toward a positive resolution.

Build a support system. Surround yourself with people who believe in you. There is strength in numbers and it is often easier to face fears and build confidence with the love and support of others.

KEEP HUMOUR AND LAUGHTER AS VITAL INGREDIENTS OF MY BUSINESS PLAN

Humour and laughter are as essential in a work environment as computers, fax machines and telephones. As stress in the workplace can sour an atmosphere and make work an unpleasant place to be, humour and laughter can bond people together like nothing else and create a happy working team. And happy people are far more efficient and productive people.

Think about it: most of us spend more time in our work environment with co-workers than any place else. Doesn't it make sense to have a relaxed, stress-free environment?

Don't forget to play. Our work days, unfortunately, no longer have play periods like we had in school. All animals play, and yet we've cut it out of our daily life. Play relieves tension and builds trust. Find appropriate ways to play at work. Maybe it's an organised game or maybe spontaneous fun. Diligence in any work place is important, but without an underlying atmosphere of play and trust, diligence becomes drudge.

It is so important in any venture to create an environment where people feel safe enough to relax and be themselves. Start a business meeting with something that will put smiles on everyone's faces. Think about how you can bring some joy into your co-workers lives. Take the first step of breaking down barriers. Surprise others with humour and good will and you'll be surprised of the rewards that are reaped in return.

Humour can be found in everything. When things get tough, when situations seem impossible, that is the best time to see the humour. Not only does it relieve the stress and tension, but it puts everything into perspective. It makes communication easier. Nothing is so important we can't laugh at it and ourselves. This is especially true in conflict. When energy between people becomes too charged, humour is always the great equaliser that enables people to find common ground and ultimately, a solution.

Never be too caught up in your work or your fear to laugh.

GET UP EARLY in the Morning

GET UP EARLY IN THE MORNING

Every new day is a new beginning. As flowers open to greet
the sun, so we open to take in the energy of the morning.
By getting up early, we are in harmony with the rhythms of
nature. Our energies are higher, our powers of concentration
are better, our abilities to tap into our consciousness
are deeper.

We are bombarded by media, information, noise and
distraction from every side. The early morning is the best
time to create a routine where you can clear away that noise.
Take this quiet time to do things you don't have time to do
during the rest of the day.

Write your dreams in your journal. Many intuitive thoughts
come through your dreams, and this is the time you are
closest to them. Open your soul and let your thoughts

flow freely. You'll be amazed at the insight and truthfulness you have during those first moments of the morning.

Meditation is easiest in the morning. Hear your inner voice, connect with your true vision, learn to trust your intuition and strengthen your higher self.

A walk in the morning often becomes a marvellous meditation. Whether you are in the city or country, the vibrancy of the morning fills the senses. Notice its freshness – the colours of the sunrise, the smells that surround you, the dew on the grass, the birds singing a morning chorus.

By rising early, you will be surprised how much more you can get accomplished. With replenished energy from a good night's sleep, you can set the tone of the day by doing your exercise, having your health drink, even get your e-mail done and by the time you've finished all that, it's still only eight in the morning.

And yes, sometimes it's hard to give ourselves morning time with all our obligations and responsibilities – husbands, partners, families, kids. But to realise our dreams, to create our visions, it is important to make simple but effective day-to-day changes. So get up half-an-hour earlier than everyone else, before the onslaught of kids and work and routine. Give the gift of early morning to yourself.

Not neglect
my
personal
Relationships,
loved ones
and

friends in any way

NOT NEGLECT MY PERSONAL RELATIONSHIPS, LOVED ONES AND FRIENDS IN ANY WAY

A new business, a growing enterprise, even a nine-to-five job, frequently becomes all consuming. All too often we allow the obstacles and stress of our workday to take over our lives. Logically, we know work is not our entire life, but just a part of it. Still, our work life tends to invade everything.

It's so important to consciously separate yourself from your work. Take work seriously, but not personally. Make sure you stay grounded by not neglecting family and friends. No matter how busy you get, take that phone call from a friend. He or she can often put a smile on your face.

Give of yourself and your time to loved ones. If you can't talk in person or by phone, keep in touch by a postcard or e-mail – it will strengthen your bond and remind you of the importance of a balanced life. Telling someone you love him or her is as wonderfully beneficial for yourself as it is for the receiver.

The balance of work, personal relationships, recreation time and time for yourself is basically about having a whole life. In starting your own business, it is always important at the beginning to ask some vital questions about how the vision you have of your personal life and business life will fit together. How and where do you want to live – city, town, or country? Do you have small children? How much time do you want to spend with them? Does it make more sense for you to work at home? To have a balanced life, you have to judge it as a whole, not in separate compartments.

Get in touch with the one person you've been thinking about for weeks, but haven't written to or called. Update them about the details of your life, but also tell them what's in your heart, and why it was important you connected with them. The reward will be yours.

MANIFEST ABUNDANCE IN ALL AREAS OF MY LIFE

Abundance is the richness of life, not just the material things. It's our relationships, our loved ones, our play, our food, our health, our spirit. Abundance is always present in nature. You can find abundance in the energy of money, but you can just as easily find it in a walk through a meadow of wildflowers or the gathering of your family around you.

WE ARE ALL CAPABLE OF MANIFESTING ABUNDANCE.

Positive thinking, focus and intention can produce just about anything. To manifest, you must be clear and precise with your intention. A failure to manifest usually is because on some level we don't think we deserve it.

In business, money is most often the yardstick of abundance. But what is money really? And what is your relationship with it? These are key questions in your ability to manifest money.

Ask yourself: Do you find it difficult in your current situation to ask for more money, either from your boss or from your partner? Do you like giving gifts but not receiving them? Do you think it's possible that on some level you don't think you deserve abundance in your life?

Beginning to view money purely as a form of energy to create your dreams is the first step towards its manifestation. If you are tied to the notion of money as material, you will be dragged down by it. Free yourself in your attitude and see if your relationship to money and how it comes to you changes.

Affirmations are often used in manifesting your desires. Affirmations are conscious statements of deep personal truths. Use affirmations as important reminders to yourself and messages to the universe. Create your own affirmations, there is tremendous power in them.

> **A SEED affirmation:** 'I add value to all areas of my life and honor my true worth. I am ready to receive all the bouquets that I deserve.'

Manifesting abundance is also about welcoming its attainment and appreciating the blessing it provides. Creating abundance is the ability to see the richness of the life you currently have and how, in turning your dreams into reality, the manifestation of your intention is ultimately a gift from the Creator. Having abundance means taking the responsibility of its grace and using it wisely.

KEEP MY CLUTTER TO A MINIMUM

KEEP MY CLUTTER TO A MINIMUM

As you would never start a journey in the thick overgrowth of a jungle, so you should never embark on a new endeavor surrounded by the clutter you've accumulated. You won't be able to see your path clearly. You'll be confused by the chaos and dragged down by the sheer weight of the junk that surrounds you.

With your new beginning, make sure you have a new clearing, both in your physical environment and your mental outlook. It takes great energy to make changes and start something new. Make your task that much easier by clearing all the clutter you can.

Start with your work place. Is your office neat and orderly? Is your desk clear of papers you don't need? Why not go through all your old files, letters, and junk mail right now and throw away everything that you know you'll never look at again.

Then organise what's left. Put important papers together in identifiable files. Sort out your financial paperwork. Collect all those phone numbers that are on business cards and bits of paper and put them onto a computer database and electronic organiser.

No need to stop at your office, either. Clear the clutter from your life as well. Starting a new phase in life often means a new look is in order too. Take a peek in your clothes cupboard. Get rid of those old clothes you never wear and think of giving yourself a new look. A different hairstyle, a change in your make-up, new clothes – they all make a difference in the way you present yourself and often do wonders for your self-esteem.

Look to all areas of your life and see where you can clear the clutter and start on renewal. Does your car need cleaning? What about your wallet or handbag? And your body? Is it time to clean a junk food habit and start eating more healthily?

The point is, when starting something new it is always a good idea to have a physical renewal that reflects your new endeavour. It really works when you clear the clutter and create a new space in which you will manifest your ideas and dreams.

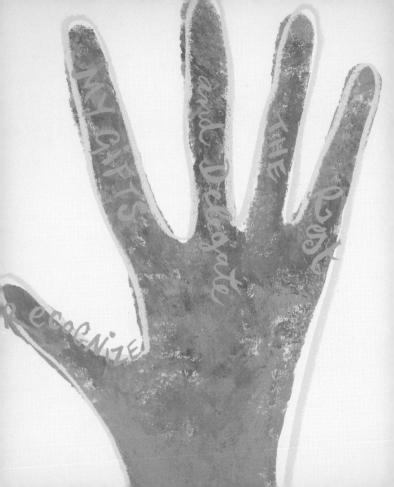

RECOGNIZE MY GIFTS AND DELEGATE THE REST

We cannot be everything for everybody. Each of us has our
different and unique gifts. One of the first lessons in business
is to take a step back, look at all areas of your life and
objectively analyse your strengths and weaknesses.

We often take for granted our strengths because they seem
so obvious and effortless to us. But these are the exact
things you should focus your time and energies on because
these are the areas where you will be most effective in and
reap the greatest rewards. What comes easily to you?
What are you good at? What makes you light up inside
when you think about doing it?

If you are unsure of what new direction you want to take or
what sort of business you want to start, ask yourself where
your passions lie. And is there a way to combine these

passions with your existing personal and professional experience and skills? Make a list of 20 activities that you currently enjoy doing the most.

Because you are your own worst critic, looking at your weaknesses may be all too easy. It's important not to judge yourself for the things you don't do well. Honestly assessing them will enable you to turn those weaknesses into positives. The way of doing this, especially in business, is to find others who are strong in those areas you are weak in.

While it is important to keep an eye on your budget when starting a business, never skimp when hiring professionals to help you in key situations. If you need financial planning, get a good accountant. Make sure your legal work is done by a competent lawyer. Hiring an expert to help you create a stellar business plan is well worth the expense if it brings in investors.

Don't be afraid to seek help or delegate tasks and
responsibilities. Just make sure that the people you are
entrusting these tasks to are capable and responsible.

LOOK AT DIFFICULT SITUATIONS FROM ALL PERSPECTIVES

The way we act is motivated by our own wishes, desires, prejudices, hopes, backgrounds, and moods. We are all full of pre-conceived notions of the way things should be and the way people should act. Sometimes it's not a bad thing – these perspectives are often the qualities that define us and are the spurs that keep us going. However, when dealing with others, in business and also in life, it is fundamental that we see all perspectives of a situation and see it as objectively and non-judgmentally as possible.

None of us hold a monopoly on absolute truth and reality. Sometimes our fears colour the way we see things. Taking into account everyone's opinion and perspective usually gives a much fuller picture of a situation than our own individual viewpoint. If you can release your tie to your own opinion, you will probably discover new and better solutions to a problem. You will also find ways of breaking through adversarial situations. When you invite people to share their opinions and then work their suggestions into solving the problem at hand, it's amazing how tension turns to cooperation and difficult problems transform into satisfying solutions.

The most difficult time to see someone else's opinion is in time of conflict. In confronting someone, you can come from a point of certainty and power or from openness and humility. Certainty and power is how we usually act in conflict. And it rarely wins any fans or converts. Openness and humility are difficult to practise in the face of conflict. Our first instinct is always to meet aggression with our own aggression. Yet if we can hold an open space and invite the other person to share their views, a meeting of the minds can take place. Often, having a third person act as referee in a conflict helps to bring out everyone's perspective and is a great way of mediating conflict.

Begin to make a habit of practising open communication. If you work with a staff, encourage everyone to be involved in the decision making. Make sure everyone has a part in establishing the values by which your company works. It's the continual bond between people that opens the channels of communication and makes everyone feel comfortable to share their opinions.

Remember to refrain from making judgments, either on yourself or other people. We all have valuable things to contribute.

Welcome in MENTors AND Mentor others in Return

WELCOME IN MENTORS AND MENTOR OTHERS IN RETURN

Mentoring is one of the most valuable tools we learn by.
Without mentors, essential knowledge might never be passed
on. To mentor a person or a group is one of the most
enjoyable things anyone can do. Mentoring is service
towards others, and in that mentoring is its own reward.
But it's also the extension of the spark, the sharing of ideas
and experience that an individual accumulates, usually
through years of toil in a specific discipline or profession.

Mentorship is often confused with guruship, and mentors are
put (or put themselves) on pedestals. This is wrong.
Mentoring is about giving and receiving. It is about being a
teacher and a student simultaneously. There is no hierarchy
in mentoring – the person doing the mentoring often gets as

much value and knowledge as they impart. Mentoring should be completely democratic. We are all each other's mentors.

In finding a mentor, you should carefully research the field you are interested in and ascertain who the leaders and experts in that field are. Read any articles or books they've published, go and hear them speak or even make an appointment to introduce yourself to them. You will be surprised how open and accessible people are to sharing their time with you. Once you find the right person, someone with whom you feel comfortable and who has the expertise you seek, *ASK HIM OR HER TO BE YOUR MENTOR*.

Don't be afraid. Asking for help is one of the most human things we can do. Don't expect mentors to volunteer to help you, you must do the asking. And don't be surprised if the person you ask is both flattered and open to the idea of becoming a mentor.

Being a mentor is inspirational and rewarding. Through the questions and problems presented to you, new light is often shed on your field that you felt so familiar with. Mentoring is not just about sharing your knowledge, but sharing your mistakes too. If you don't know something, don't pretend you do – become the student and find the answer together.

Group networks, such as the SEED Community, are a way of mutually mentoring, sharing and exchanging advice and practical needs. They provide a connection to potential allies and partners, customers, suppliers, neighbourhood and national organisations and even competitors. The wider your network of connections through mentors and group networks becomes, the greater your knowledge and your chance for success.

LIGHT CANDLES EVERYDAY AND SURROUND MYSELF WITH FRESH FLOWERS

Lighting a candle is a prayer. It is a reaffirmation of life.
By lighting candles every day, you observe a ritual of renewal
that will serve as a reminder of the heat, the passion, the
beauty of life. Start your day by lighting a candle. Watch it
burn, let your mind dance with the flickering flame, let the
warmth and glow of the candle fill your spirit. In that
moment, your daily problems will fade and your connection
with the spirit that burns inside of you will fill you with
what's really important – the pure joy and love of being alive.
Let the candle burn continually so that during a hectic
working day you have a reminder, a place to go to gather
and renew your strength.

Surround yourself with fresh flowers because they are
beautiful, smell wonderful, are refreshing and inspiring and,

like the candle, will fill your soul with joy. Flowers are beauty that springs from the earth, they are natural and organic, they are infused with the same life force that we are and they provide pure delight through their existence. In their beauty they can serve as a metaphor for you and your enterprise – something that brings joy and value into the world.

Bring this practice into your work place. Put flowers all around the office. Light a candle with those you work with. Create a ritual and say a prayer with the lighting. It will create an immediate connection and bring everyone together. Taking the time for such a simple, yet effective ritual, creates a flow between people where masks fall away and open and honest connections are made.

If you can't physically light a candle every day, start your day by ritually lighting one in your mind. If you can't afford fresh flowers, take a walk through a garden or park and soak in the colours and smells of the blossoms around you.

The important thing is to get in the daily habit of seeing life and beauty everywhere. It's about consciously creating life-affirming environments and values. With this practice, these values will take root within you and your outlook on life and your business will shine with the same radiance as the candles and flowers.

GIVE PEOPLE MORE THAN THEY EXPECT

When you get an unexpected gift from someone, doesn't it usually delight you? Similarly, when someone surprises you with an effort that is more than you ask for or offers a new perspective that is especially insightful, doesn't that delight you in a similar way?

Giving people more than they expect doesn't necessarily mean you have to work harder or give things away. It means making the effort to stay open, be present, connect fully and give totally. It is about giving of your true self in an unconditional way.

Conversely, when you have expectations from others and don't communicate with them properly, you are setting yourself up for disappointment. Be clear and up front in telling others what you expect from them. As it is important to be present in accessing what others need, so too it is equally important to be clear and present in expressing your own needs to others. Don't expect that they know what you want. And don't project your expectations on others and assume they will happen. It just doesn't work that way.

Sometimes people won't even recognise your extra effort. If your effort was given to be recognised, you will be let down. But if you get in the habit of giving more than people expect, your good efforts will ultimately be appreciated and you will receive a greater reward than you imagined, often in very surprising ways.

Looking at your efforts and work as service and not solely as a moneymaking endeavour will entirely change your attitude towards work and increase the rewards you get from it. You will have more energy, more connection and definitely more joy when you feel you are giving of yourself for good. You will have a reason and inspiration to get up in the morning.

Begin today by truly meeting people with your entire being. Listen to what they are saying. Focus on what they want. Pay attention to their needs. And don't hold back with what you have to offer. Make this a habit and the extra effort becomes effortless.

talk SLOWLY

but think quickly

TALK SLOWLY BUT THINK QUICKLY

Words are powerful. What you say reflects on who you are and how you conduct yourself in the world. If we are to utilise the power of our words, we must learn to use them effectively and responsibly.

It happens to all of us: something slips out of our mouths that we immediately regret saying. It happens in business situations and during personal conversations. It often happens in the heat of an argument, sometimes in casual conversations, too often when we gossip.

One good way of learning to consciously express what you're really thinking through words is to keep a journal. Journal writing is essentially letting your inner being talk in a free, unedited way. It's a conversation with yourself where you are both listening and talking.

Journal writing not only helps you keep track of intuitive ideas, but is also a way to overcome any creative blocks. Writing in a journal daily gets you in touch with yourself by letting your thoughts form freely on the page. It gives you a sense of what it is to think quickly.

By writing your thoughts and perceptions in words, it gets you in the practice of focusing these thoughts into coherent language.

Journal writing is a great tool for touching into both your conscious and unconscious self. It is highly recommended.

What you'll learn from journal writing is not to edit yourself, but rather, how to pay full attention to the conversation. Next time you're talking with someone, stop for a moment and ask yourself if you are really present. When you talk, be sure to breathe. Don't be afraid to pause for a moment before going onto the next thought. Most importantly, be aware of what you're talking about; don't let the aimless chatter of your mind control your tongue. Let your words flow from a place of concentration and true consciousness.

WHEN I LOSE, DON'T LOSE THE LESSON

Successful people often fail. Winners often lose. What separates those who take their losses and turn them into triumphs and those who linger in the depths of defeat is the ability to look hard at why they failed and learn from it.

Notice the behaviour of small children. When they fall over they don't ponder their failure, they just pick themselves up and start again. We still have that ability in us. Picking ourselves up and moving forward is the key to success *if* we absorb the lesson in our failure and try not to repeat it. Moving forward and making the same mistake over and over again will only lead to disillusionment and defeat.

What stops us from going forward or absorbing the lesson is always fear. Fear that we'd fail again. Fear of really analysing why something didn't work because we'd discover our shortcomings.

Failure really is just a matter of perspective. What, in the short term, seems devastating, often, in the long term, turns out to be the best thing that could have happened. More often than not, the first setbacks are the keys that provide the spark to success. Don't be afraid to get upset about failure – it's only natural to be dispirited. Once you realise that initial failure is just a part of the process of attaining your goal, your perspective on losing will change. Overcome your fear, face your losses with courage, and take action to turn the losses into a lesson and you'll be amazed how your fortunes will change.

With women's enterprises especially, there have always been initial obstacles and setbacks. Traditional investment avenues remain suspicious and banks are hesitant to give qualified women loans. It's doubly important for woman not to take defeat personally.

> *The lesson here is to look towards innovative new ways of doing business.*

Bartering our services (like Womanshare and Barter Business Network.com), banding together in women's banking and investment consortiums and having a network of women entrepreneurs sharing information and services (SEED), are all new, alternative, feminine ways of doing business.

KNOW MY INDUSTRY

You know your interests, you are aware of your strengths and weaknesses and your intuition points you strongly in one direction. Now it's imperative for you to do research in the industry you're interested in.

Don't be naïve in thinking you know all about an industry if you don't have experience in it. If your chosen field truly excites you, the research should be fun, almost like a treasure hunt. And where do you start this hunt?

- Read the business section of your local and national newspapers on a daily basis. Keep an eye out for articles on new businesses and entrepreneurs and anything that pertains to your potential area of business.

- Go to your local library. Find appropriate magazines and trade publications of your prospective business.

- Search through the Internet. It is a treasure chest in itself of pertinent information, contacts and links. If you don't own a computer, use one in your office, the library or even a cyber-café.

- Find out if there are any industry-related conferences or trade shows near where you live and try to attend. This is a great way to get solid, professional information about your industry and also make key contacts that can be useful to you.

- Talk to people in the industry. Ask them how they got started, what kind of background, experience and funding they had. Find out what hardships they've survived and why they love what they do.

- Find a mentor within your chosen industry.

- Research by doing. Nothing beats first hand experience.
  If possible, get a job in the field you're interested in.
  See what the reality of the industry is from the inside.

Don't be discouraged by what you don't know. Focus on
grounding yourself in reality without losing your enthusiasm
and confidence. A little knowledge goes a long way. More
knowledge gives you the tools to be successful. You can
never know too much or be too experienced.

KEEP IMPROVING MY TECHNOLOGY SKILLS

This is the era of technology. You can't do business today
without being technologically proficient. Old technologies
seem to be transforming into something different every few
months and innovative, new technologies are appearing in
the work place everyday. Sometimes it seems overwhelming
to keep up with the pace of change.

Don't be overwhelmed. Remember, these new technologies
are just tools to enable you to make your life more
manageable and your work more orderly and efficient. If
kids can handle the new technologies, so can you. Learn to
embrace all that is new and you'll most likely discover
something wonderful and fun.

The most widespread new technologies are, of course, the
computer and the Internet. If you don't know how to work a

computer, learn. Sign up for a computer course, get a friend
(or your child) to teach you, or sit down with an instruction
book and teach yourself. Computers can be unnerving and
incredibly frustrating, especially in the beginning. But once
you master the basics – and you will with a little practice – it
will become the most valuable tool you have.

In your business, your computer
should contain your database of
contacts and all your financial
information. Various programs
will help you create letter
formats, do spread sheets,
financial forecasts, produce
graphics, and much more.
E-mail is essential in today's
business world. It is an accepted standard for almost all
business correspondence today. It is convenient and even

fun, enabling you to be in close and easy contact with business associates, customers, family and friends.

The Internet is equally invaluable. It is a gateway to knowledge, people and organisations. Most trade organisations have website addresses, as do trade publications, and almost every industry has Internet sites to link into. There are also women entrepreneur organisations as well as small business networks.

Having a website for your business is almost a requirement today. You can design one yourself or hire experts who'll put together everything from simple, one-page sites to elaborate, multi-linked sites. If your business requires new technology that you do not have expertise in, it is always best to hire a consultant to put together a package for you.

This era of technology is here to stay. Make it your friend.

smile when picking up the phone

SMILE WHEN PICKING UP THE PHONE

Why smile? No one sees you pick up the phone and say 'hello'. It seems silly to put on a smile for such a small and seemingly inconsequential act.

But try it. A smile can be heard over the phone, because attitude is reflected in the voice. And a smile in the voice is an invitation, a true greeting for the person on the other end of the line to be met. You'd be surprised at how much the 'good vibrations' in an inviting voice can set the tone of a conversation.

The phone is a disembodying device and a smile adds to the human warmth, immediately setting the tone of a conversation. It can put the other party at ease. It can make the difference between a productive conversation and one that may be strained. In personal calls, it invites openness

and honesty as opposed to guardedness and ambiguity.
In business, it could even make the difference between a
sale or not.

By smiling when you pick up the phone you are also
consciously altering your patterned way of doing things.
By taking that mindful moment to smile, you put yourself in
a state of awareness where you can more easily effect your
attitude and the attitude of all you come in contact with.
In our workplaces especially, we can easily get lost in our
heads. By consciously bringing in positive energy through the
single act of smiling when you pick up the phone, you can
literally transform your own state of being.

The smile doesn't have to stop when you hang up the phone.
You can take your positive energy and literally change the
atmosphere of your environment. Smile when you deal with
people in your office. Try it on your husband, partner or kids.

Communication is 80 percent body language. A smile often communicates more than 10 thousand words. A smile lights up any situation and puts everyone at ease.

Smile and the whole world smiles with you. It really works.

REMEMBER MY BODY IS MY MOST IMPORTANT TOOL – STRETCH, EXERCISE, BREATHE, GO FOR A WALK, DANCE

Getting enough exercise is a major challenge in our modern world. Between family, friends and work, there's never enough time to make exercise a convenient part of the day. And if you're starting a business – working long hours, often over a hot computer, with stressful situations hovering around – it's even worse.

But getting exercise and keeping your body fit is probably the most important thing you can do to effect a healthy balance and maintain effective work stamina. Investing in your body will return valuable dividends many times over. Whether it's an early gym session, regular massage or yoga practice, it's absolutely crucial to stay conscious of your body's need to stretch, move and relax.

Stretch in your workplace

Brain refresher – sitting in your chair at your desk, bringing your upper body towards the floor. Hold as the blood rushes to the brain, bringing essential oxygen.

Head rolls – slowly roll your head to the left in a circular motion. If you hear soft clicks, it means your neck is loosening up.

Shoulder shrugs – raise your shoulders to your ears and hold for three seconds. Repeat several times.

Exercise/walk

If you can't get to a gym for a workout regimen, take a walk – the more vigorous the better. Let go of work during this interlude. Be conscious of your surroundings. Feel your body enjoy the pure physicalness of walking. Turn it into a walking meditation. Make this a regular part of the day and see how it invigorates your body and mind.

Breathe

Bring in new energy, expel old negativity. Take five slow breaths in, hold for a moment then release. Close your eyes and concentrate on the air entering your nose, filling your lungs. Visualise these breaths as white light, rejuvenating your body and spirit. Repeat four times a day.

Dance

Dance is an essential part of all indigenous cultures. It fills our modern souls too, though in many ways we've lost our essential tie to it. Dancing is an expression of joy and everyone can dance. If you're shy about dancing, go into a room by yourself, turn on some music with a rhythm you like, close your eyes and let go. Melt into the music with the movement of your body. Don't think, feel.

Treat your body with love and respect, it's your gift to yourself.

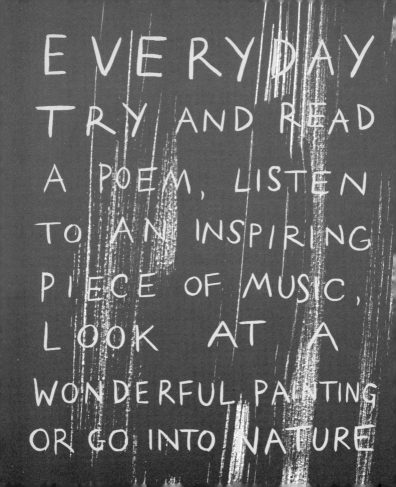

EVERY DAY
TRY AND READ
A POEM, LISTEN
TO AN INSPIRING
PIECE OF MUSIC,
LOOK AT A
WONDERFUL PAINTING
OR GO INTO NATURE

EVERY DAY TRY AND READ A POEM, LISTEN TO AN INSPIRING PIECE OF MUSIC, LOOK AT A WONDERFUL PAINTING OR GO INTO NATURE

Bringing beauty into our lives on a daily basis is as important as keeping our body well tuned. Our hearts continually need lifting. Our souls always take nourishment from inspiration. It's easy to neglect what seems to be a luxury. Beauty and inspiration are not luxuries though; they are as meaningful to us as a drink of water or a loaf of bread.

Beauty reminds us of the wonderment of being alive. Inspiration gives us our reason to work and play.

Make time for beauty and inspiration in your life. Even if it's only for 10 minutes a day. Carry a favourite book of poetry or inspirational pieces and open it when you are waiting in a line. Take a walk in nature by finding a secluded park or a wooded trail on the outskirts of town. Set aside an hour or two to go to a museum. Look to see if there are any noontime concerts where you can slip away for lunch. The key to putting beauty in your life is making the effort to do it.

Once you've made that effort, it's important to let the beauty and inspiration in. It's astonishing how much we constrain and filter everything that is around us. Open your eyes and look as if you're seeing something for the first time. Free your ears from their filters and let the sounds that surround you pour in. There are miracles everywhere. A column of ants working together to carry crumbs to their nest is amazing. The architecture of many city buildings, both old and modern, are awe inspiring when you study them closely. The wind swirling through tall grass is as musical as the string section of the finest symphony orchestra.

*Keep open and the world will enliven
you in unexpected ways. Inspiration is in
everything and every moment. See it. Let it
fill you up. And don't be surprised if you
are inspired with a great new idea.*

DRINK SIX TO EIGHT GLASSES OF PURE WATER EVERY DAY

Our bodies are more than two-thirds water. Water is literally the key component of our lifeblood. It is our thermostat, keeping our body temperature constant. We lose water every living moment. Our breath exhales moisture and water constantly passes through our skin. And of course, we lose water through urination. Without continually replenishing our water, we die. So it makes sense that getting water, enough water, is essential to our existence.

It is an established fact that six to eight glasses of water daily is what's required to flush out the toxins from our system and replenish, refresh and keep our bodies functioning at their maximum capabilities.

Drinking enough water is essential for our beauty as well as our health.

- Skin needs to be constantly hydrated to be and look healthy.
- Though you can lose weight by dehydrating yourself, fat cannot be eliminated without water – it's obviously dangerous to drink less for weight control.
- Headaches have been directly linked to dehydration.

Obviously, water should be as pure as possible. The less additives and chemicals the better. Bottled water is usually a safer bet than tap water. And water in its purest form is far better than when we add to it. Tea and coffee taste great and offer a sure pick up, but they are full of caffeine, which works to deplete rather than replenish the system. If you must drink these or other drinks (sodas, sports drinks, fruit flavoured juices), do it in moderation. With no calories and no fat, water remains the king of healthy drinks.

Water is also a metaphor for the giving and sustaining of life. We water our plants to grow. We water our souls for enlightenment. We water our businesses for success.

Surround yourself with moving water. Next time you're near a brook or river take a moment and let the sound wash over you. Better yet, jump in and experience the wonderful sensation of water over your skin. If you can, get a fountain for your home – the calming sound of gently running water is incredibly relaxing. Start your meditation on the image and sound of a river or waterfall.

Water is, in every respect, the great giver of life. So plunge in and drink up. Cheers!

LISTEN AS WELL AS TALK

The ability to listen is one of the best traits anyone can have. We've all met people who have that ability – their eyes focus sharply on us, we can feel their energy as they seem to be 100 percent present, soaking up what we have to say and often giving back an insightful response. We usually feel honored when someone is giving us his or her complete attention. We almost always like the person that listens well. And for good reason: the good listener is giving us a gift by providing us with one of our most basic human needs – the need to communicate and be understood.

When we listen well, we gain an understanding of the person who is talking and, if we're lucky, the knowledge and wisdom that person has to offer. Even if it doesn't seem apparent, everyone has something valuable to offer when they speak. Sometimes it's just the knowledge of how to communicate with that person; sometimes it's a key to insight, a solution to a problem, or the spark of inspiration.

More often than not, people who talk without listening are trying to prove how smart they are, how much they know. But the good listeners are the smart ones – they're open to learning something, they don't seem like fools by running on at the mouth, and they make a bond of trust that is as valuable in business as it is in personal relationships.

Unfortunately, most of us are not great listeners. Our minds often wander when we listen. Sometimes they wander to what we're going to say, sometimes they are running in a thousand different directions, none of which has anything to do with the conversation at hand.

Never assume you know the point the person is trying to make. And even if you do, let them finish what they are saying. For a conversation to be open and free flowing, people need to feel they are being heard. You'll be pleasantly surprised how much more people will listen to you when you listen to them.

LEARN THE RULES THEN BREAK SOME

Mae West said: 'When I'm good, I'm very very good. And when I'm bad, I'm better.' Mae West knew the rules. She knew the morals and mores of her time; she also knew the new 'street' attitudes of the Roaring Twenties and was the first to openly break her society's taboos by brazenly flaunting a woman's sexuality.

Her lesson though was not so much to trample on the rules, but to dare to do something that was both honest and different. She presented a picture of women that resonated with her world far better than the puritanical ideal of what a woman was 'supposed to be'. By breaking the rules, she found truth and became one of the most famous women of her time and remains an enduring icon.

Breaking the rules is about changing patterns and unlocking the truths that are inside all of us. We all get into routines. Routines and patterns are not bad things in themselves. But when we begin living our lives by rote, we often stop moving forward. We become rigid in our ways.

Breaking the rules does not mean going wild and getting rid of all structure or boundaries. Nor does it mean going against core values – no need to relive our rebellious adolescence again. Breaking the rules means shaking things up, changing your behavioural patterns so you can see your life with fresh eyes and act with a new sense of unbounded freedom.

When you break a rule, be conscious of doing it. If you take a day off work, do something constructive and fun like painting a picture or going to a museum. If you walk where it says 'No Trespassing', do it through a field of wild flowers. Break free purposefully.

Most importantly, don't be afraid to break the rules. Leaders break the rules. Artists break the rules. Inventors break the rules. Entrepreneurs break the rules. Know what you're breaking and why – then go ahead and pull out all the stops.

NOTHING IS MORE SEXY THAN CONFIDENCE

Confidence draws people like flowers draw bees. Confidence is the biggest personal asset you can have. If you're truly confident about your business, chances are you will be successful. If you're truly confident in life, chances are good things will continually happen to you. Positive energy attracts positive energy. When manifesting your vision into reality, you must be confident you can succeed.

The problem is, confidence does not just happen by magic. All of us, even the seemingly most confident people in the world, are filled with doubts. With women especially, low self-esteem runs rampant. We underestimate ourselves. We live in a world where the media, fashion and advertising industries tell us how flawed we are. They tell us if only we use a certain perfume or lipstick, dress in a particular fashion or pout our lips in a particular way, only then will we be sexy and beautiful. Nonsense!

We are all beautiful. We are all sexy. Our responsibility is to realise it and get past the rubbish that is fed to us by the marketing companies. We all come in different shapes, sizes and colours. Our bond is the uniqueness each one of us brings to this world. Once we get in touch with the exquisite soul inside us, our confidence will radiate like a thousand-watt light bulb.

If you lack confidence or self esteem in any way, make a resolution to confront the problem. Take action. Find a group of friends with whom you can openly and non-judgmentally share problems and swap wisdom. Sharing with others always helps build confidence. Supporting and nurturing is the feminine way of building confidence.

The most empowering thing you can do is take active steps to build your confidence. Once you've found it inside of you, where it's always been, take a look in the mirror: you'll see a face that knows what sexiness is about.

REMEMBER THAT NO-ONE, NOT EVEN I AM PERFECT, BUT I'M DOING THE BEST I CAN

Though I am not perfect, my intention is.
Though I don't always reach my goal, I never give less than my best.
If my words and actions come from my heart, I have nothing to regret.
If my actions are pure, then my success – regardless of outcome – is guaranteed.

We are all human. We all have failings and we all make mistakes. There is no score card in life though. Acknowledging our failings then overcoming them is what makes the challenge of life worth living.

We face a wide variety of obstacles every day. Our jobs are filled with difficulties to be overcome. Our personal and home lives are a mixture of pleasures to be enjoyed and problems to be solved. Money, children, school, appointments, dinners, obligations – often the problems seem overwhelming. Proper perspective is sometimes difficult to maintain as we get lost in the 'stuff' of life. That's why it's important to consciously take a few minutes at the beginning of your day to pause for some quiet time.

It is during that time you'll be able to see the bigger picture and bring yourself to the pure intentions of your actions.

If you operate from a state of purity and grace, the problems and obstacles placed in front of you lose their negative charge. Acceptance is knowing that you did your best and that any mistakes you may have made are only building blocks to your success. Perfection, when rarely achieved, is fleeting. Giving your true and best effort is a practice that will bring you satisfaction for a lifetime.

At the core of all of us is the fact that we are tied together by our humanity, that we share the same desire of happiness for ourselves and our families, and that, if we searched our inner hearts, we'd find our best efforts are given through our higher selves. The feminine way of doing business and living life is about the integration of our higher selves into our daily lives.

Seed Contacts

INTERNATIONAL

Business and Professional Women International
Studio 16, Cloisters Business Centre
8 Battersea Park Road, London SW8 4BG
England
Tel: 44(171) 738-8323
Fax: 44(171) 622-8528

www.bpwintl.com

email: bpwihq@cs.com

Center for International Private Enterprise (CIPE)
1155 15th Street, NW, Suite 700,
Washington, DC 20005 USA
Tel: (202) 721-9200
Fax: (202) 721-9250

www.cipe.org/prog/women

email: cipe@cipe.org

CIPE IS AN AFFILIATE OF THE US
CHAMBER OF COMMERCE.

Les Femmes Chefs d'Enterprises Mondial (FCEM) The World Association of Women Entrepreneurs
Leyla Khaiat, FCEM President
17, Rue Abderrahman el Jaziri,1002
Tunis Belvedere Tunisia
Tel: (216) 179-3432
Fax: (202) 721-9250

email: plastiss@planet.tn

Arline Woutersz, FCEM Vice President
114 Gloucester Place, London WIH 3DB UK
Tel/Fax: (171) 935-0085

email: woutersz@msn.com

Phyllis Hill Slater, FCEM Vice President
45 North Station Plaza, Suite L/100,
Great Neck, NY 11021 USA
Tel: (516) 773.7779
Fax: (516) 773.7729

email: hillslater@aol.com

United Nations Development Fund for Women
304 East 45th Street, 15th Floor,
New York, NY 10017 USA
Tel: (212) 906 6400
Fax: (212) 906 6705

www.unifem.undp.org

email: unifem@undp.org

UNIFEM PROMOTES WOMEN'S EMPOWER-
MENT AND GENDER EQUALITY. IT WORKS
TO ENSURE THE PARTICIPATION OF
WOMEN IN ALL LEVELS OF DEVELOPMENT
PLANNING AND PRACTICE, AND ACTS AS
A CATALYST WITHIN THE UN SYSTEM,
SUPPORTING EFFORTS THAT LINK THE
NEEDS AND CONCERNS OF WOMEN TO
ALL CRITICAL ISSUES ON THE NATIONAL,
REGIONAL AND GLOBAL AGENDAS.

ASIA

www.womenasia.com

Rosemary Brisco
76 Cape Hatteras Court
Redwood City, CA USA 94065
Tel: (650) 654-6926
Fax: (650) 654-6927

email: info@womenasia.com

THEY ARE A BUSINESS TO BUSINESS NET-
WORK CONNECTING WOMEN IN ASIA AND
NORTH AMERICA FOR THE PURPOSE OF
TRADE AND COMMERCE.

AUSTRALIA

Australian Federation of Business and Professional Women

PO Box 1267 Swan Hill, VIC 3585
Tel/Fax: (035) 032-0068

www.bpw.com.au

email: bpwaust@bpw.com.au

BPW AUSTRALIA CO-OPERATES WITH
BUSINESS AND PROFESSIONAL WOMEN

IN OTHER COUNTRIES TO ENCOURAGE
INTERNATIONAL UNDERSTANDING AND
PROVIDES A FORUM FOR THE
DISCUSSIONS OF INTERNATIONAL,
NATIONAL, STATE, AND LOCAL ISSUES

Council of Small Business Organisations of Australia (COSBOA)

Tel: 61 (0) 26273 2828
Fax: 61 (0) 26273 2222

email: rob@cosboa.com.au

NEW ZEALAND

Women's Business Network New Zealand

PO Box 2900, Wellington
Tel: 64 4 477 3564
Fax: 64 4 477 6324
Convenor: Janet Chambers

email: inquiries@womens-business.org.nz

WISE Women Network Trust

National Office, PO Box 1644, Whangarei
Tel: (09) 438 4616
Fax: (09) 438 4617

email: trustoffice@wisewomen.org.nz

ARE YOU SELF-EMPLOYED AND NEED
SOME SUPPORT? THAT'S WHAT WE ARE
HERE FOR!

CANADA

Canadian Women's Business Network

3995 MacIsaac Drive, Nanaimo, BC,
V9T 3V5
Tel: 250-741-0947

www.cdnbiz.women.com

MEXICO

Del Verbo Emprender

Salo Grabinsky

Fuente de Piramides 20 P.B. Local B

Tecamachalco, Edo. De Mexico 539350

Mexico

Tel: (525) 294-8407

www.internet.com.nx/empresas/emprender

AL SERVICIO DE LOS EMPRENDADORES Y
LA EMPRESA FAMILIAR.
HELPING LATIN AMERICAN AND HISPANIC
ENTREPRENEURS.

UNITED KINGDOM

Council on Economic Priorities (CEP)

38 Ebury Street, London SW1WOLU

Tel: 44(171) 730-2646

Fax: 44(171) 730-2664

www.cepaa.org

THE COUNCIL ON ECONOMIC PRIORITIES'
MISSION IS TO PROVIDE ACCURATE AND
IMPARTIAL ANALYSIS OF CORPORATE SOCIAL
AND ENVIRONMENTAL PERFORMANCE AND
TO PROMOTE EXCELLENCE IN CORPORATE
CITIZENSHIP. FOUNDED IN 1969.

**European Federation of Black Women
Business Owners**

Suite One, Two Tunstall Rd., London SW9
8DA

Tel: 44(171) 978 9488

Fax: 44(171) 978 9490

www.blacknet.co.uk/womeninbusiness

email: asapcoms@dircon.co.uk

Social Venture Network (Europe)

4, Great James Street

London WC1N 3DA

Tel: (171) 881-9007

Fax: (171) 881-9008

www.svneurope.org

SOCIAL VENTURE NETWORK IS AN ASSOCIA-
TION OF COMPANIES AND INDIVIDUAL BUSI-
NESS LEADERS WHO BELIEVE THEY
CAN-AND MUST-MAKE A SIGNIFICANT CON-
TRIBUTION TO SOLVE SOCIAL AND ENVIRON-
MENTAL PROBLEMS LOCALLY AND GLOBALLY.

Network for Successful UK Women

94A Holland Road, Willesden, London
NW10 5AY

Tel: (181) 963-1481

Fax: (181) 961-7468

www.networkwomenuk.org

email: netwomen@enterprise.net

**The British Association of Women
Entrepreneurs (BAWE)**

Arline Woutersz, President

114 Gloucester Place, London WIH 3DB UK

Tel/Fax: (171) 935-0085

email: woutersz@msn.com

USEFUL WOMEN'S WEBSITES

Advancing Women

www.advancingwomen.com

INTERNATIONAL BUSINESS & CAREER
COMMUNITY. NEWS, NETWORKING &
STRATEGY FOR WOMEN

Beme.com

www.beme.com

ONLINE MAGAZINE COMMUNITY WITH
MANY CHANNELS, COVERING A RANGE OF
ISSUES SUCH AS HEALTH, BEAUTY AND
LIFESTYLE.

ChannelHealth.com

www.channelhealth.com

EVERTHING YOU NEED TO KNOW ABOUT
YOUR BODY

Handbag.com

www.handbag.com

A WOMEN'S WEBSITE MAGAZINE WITH
EVERYTHING FROM RELATIONSHIPS TO
HEALTH, FASHION TO FINANCE

Independent Means

126 Powers Ave., Santa Barbara, CA
93103
Tel: (800) 350-1816

www.independentmeans.com

A RESOURCE AND SUPPORT WEBSITE FOR
YOUNG WOMEN ENTREPRENEURS

iVillage.com

www.ivillage.com

WITHIN IVILLAGE.COM, THERE IS A COM-
MUNITY FOR EVERY INTEREST, AND LINKS
TO MORE THAN 50 EXPERTS, THOUSANDS
OF MESSAGE BOARDS, AND CONSTANT
ACCESS TO A VOLUNTEER NETWORK OF
1,000+ "COMMUNITY LEADERS"

Small Business Administration

www.sba.gov

THE SMALL BUSINESS ADMINISTRATION
IS RICH WITH INFORMATION ON HOW TO
START YOUR BUSINESS AND HAS OFFICES
IN PRACTICALLY EVERY STATE IN THE US.
GO TO THIS WEBSITE TO LEARN WHICH
ONES ARE CLOSEST TO YOU AND SO
MUCH MORE. GO TO ONLINE WOMEN'S
BUSINESS CENTER FOR MORE INFO.

women.com

www.Women.com

WITH THE COMBINED STRENGTH OF
WOMEN.COM, HOMEARTS, ASTRONET,
AND HEARST'S PORTFOLIO OF WOMEN'S
MAGAZINE SITES, WOMEN.COM NETWORKS
HAS THE LARGEST BREADTH OF RESOURCES
OF ANY ONLINE WOMEN'S NETWORK.

wwwomen.com

www.wwwomen.com

THE MOST INCLUSIVE UP-TO-DATE
SEARCH SITE FOR WOMEN'S TOPICS.
THEIR TEAM OF ONLINE SURFERS HAVE
COMPILED ONE OF THE MOST COMPRE-
HENSIVE LISTS POSSIBLE.

LYNNE FRANKS founded her first company when she was twenty-one. After twenty highly successful years she sold her firm to focus on using her communications skills to encourage partnership between business and society. Leaving her London-based agency in 1992, Franks travelled the world interacting with multinationals, nation states, NGOs, and grass roots organisations.

She created the event 'What Women Want' to draw attention to the changing position of women in society, prior to attending the Beijing women's conference; she chaired the UK's first women's radio station and has become a spokesperson on women's issues and socially responsible business practices.

Lynne Franks is currently developing SEED–Sustainable Enterprise Empowerment Dynamics, a network aimed at training and empowering, particularly with regard to sustainable enterprise. She is also founder of Globalfusion, a communications consultancy organisation dedicated to making a positive difference in society through 'new marketing' – connecting people, ideas, businesses and development. She divides her time between California, the UK, and Spain.

ANN FIELD'S award-winning collages and bright illustrations are universally recognised to inspire. Her clients include Levi's Jeans for women, Hard Rock Hotel and Barneys New York. She lives in Southern California.